This copy of

THE SPARROW BOOK OF
RECORD-BREAKERS
by Pamela Cleaver

belongs to

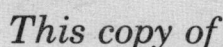
Scott Tobin

The Sparrow Book of
Record-Breakers

Pamela Cleaver

Cover illustration by John Miller
Text illustrations by Ross

A Sparrow Book
Published by Arrow Books Limited
3 Fitzroy Square, London W1P 6JD

An imprint of the Hutchinson Publishing Group

London Melbourne Sydney Auckland
Wellington Johannesburg and agencies
throughout the world

First published 1981
© Pamela Cleaver 1981

Every endeavour has been made by the author and publisher to ensure the accuracy of the records contained in this book at the time of going to press. However, new records are being set all the time and old ones discovered so neither the author nor the publisher can guarantee the accuracy of the records or accept liability for any errors.

This book is sold subject to the condition that it shall not, by way of trade or otherwise, be lent, resold, hired out, or otherwise circulated without the publisher's prior consent in any form of binding or cover other than that in which it is published and without a similar condition including this condition being imposed on the subsequent purchaser

Set in Linoterm Century
by Rowland Phototypesetting Ltd
Bury St Edmunds, Suffolk

Made and printed in Great Britain
by The Anchor Press Ltd, Tiptree, Essex

ISBN 0 09 926010 7

To the memory of my grandfathers
who stimulated my curiosity about unusual facts
when I was a child

Contents

Introduction	9
1 Children at school	13
2 Children at war	23
3 Children in government	32
4 Children in the church	40
5 Children outside the law	43
6 Children on stage and screen	49
7 Children in the arts	57
8 Children in sport	64
9 Odds and ends	76

Introduction

This is a book of records with a difference. There are many books of records available but there has never been one devoted to records set by children and written for children themselves. So here it is – the first book of children's records!

Children who qualify for inclusion in the book are drawn from throughout history and they have all done something extraordinary, interesting, or unusual before the age of sixteen and they have all been the youngest or first child to do that thing. As I began to search through piles of books to discover what records had been set by children, I found an enormous number of fascinating firsts and youngests – from the youngest highwayman to the first child to have a book published. But there were also maddening gaps. I wandered round distractedly asking people questions like 'Who was the youngest witch?' (I never found the answer to that one) and 'Where can I find out who was the youngest person to win a Victoria Cross' (that was easy to discover). I also pestered my children, buttonholing them to tell them who was the youngest smuggler and asking them what sort of youngest and firsts they would like to know about. I am grateful to Digby, Louise, Bella and Rupert for their patience with me when I was, to use their phrase about me when I am writing 'in a world of my own'.

The more books I read, the more I realised that children's lives were very different in the past. The conditions in which they lived were not as comfortable as today. They were punished more harshly both at home and at school and more was expected of them. They began to work for their living much earlier and death and pain were much more familiar to them than to children nowadays. Modern children generally have easier lives, more time to call their own and more time for growing up.

Sporting records in the book do not start until the nineteenth century. Many of the games and sports of today were not played until then and records were not kept so carefully in the past.

An enormous amount of research has gone into the book and it is as accurate as I can make it. But records are being broken every day so a book like this is never completely up-to-date. Also there will be records set by children in areas that I have not even thought about! So if you know of any new records set by children under sixteen or of any records not included in the book write to tell me for the next edition of The Sparrow Book of Record Breakers.

In my research I used four libraries and would like to thank Jon Simmons and his staff at Hertford Library, Den Reeder and his staff at Hoddesdon Library, Jack Edwards and his staff at Cheshunt Library and the librarians at the London Library. I am also grateful to the people who answered my queries: the Automobile Association, the Blue Peter Office at the BBC, Paul Buswell of the British Chess

Federation, Peter J. Lee, Ernest Wilson, Joan Butler, Lillian Siddall, David Manser, to my husband and children who gave me ideas and leads to follow up and to my publisher Caroline Sheldon who was endlessly helpful.

So all there is to say now is, here it is – The Sparrow Book of Record-Breakers – I hope you will have as much fun reading it as I had writing it.

Pamela Cleaver.

Pamela Cleaver
1980

1
Children at school

The first schoolboys

The first boys to attend school in England were the pupils of King's School Canterbury, which was founded in AD 598. The school was attached to the church built by Saint Augustine and it was given its name after the dissolution of the monasteries, when several old monastic schools took the new name, 'King's School'.

The first schoolgirls

The first girls to attend school in England were the girls of Christ's Hospital in 1552. There were only very few girls in the school and the subjects it was thought fit they should learn were very limited – reading, the Bible and sewing. This bare minimum of education was for many years considered to be enough for girls. Even by the seventeenth century, when girl's boarding schools were set up, the curriculum would be made up of such subjects as art, music, dancing, deportment, needlework and a little French conversation. It was not until 1848, when the

Governesses' Benevolent Association opened Queen's College in Harley Street for 'ladies over twelve', that girls began to receive a full education.

The first exam

The formal school exam is a modern invention.

The boys of Shrewsbury school in 1818 were the first schoolchildren to sit an exam and they were tested both orally and in writing. Schoolboys everywhere were probably dismayed by the speed at which the idea caught on. In 1850 a College of Preceptors was set up to monitor external exams at several schools. Thus the forerunners of today's O and A level exams came into being.

The first school uniforms

School uniforms were worn long before formal exams came into being. The pupils of Christ's Hospital were the first children to wear a school uniform in England. The school was opened in 1552 to accommodate 500 poor orphans in the City of London. At first all the pupils were dressed in a uniform of russet brown but the Easter after the school was set up this was changed to blue. The boys have worn this uniform ever since and are known by the nickname 'the bluecoat boys'.

The first smoking in schools

The first and probably the only boys who have been *made* to smoke at school were the schoolboys of Eton in 1660. Smoking was made compulsory in the school and those who did not take up the habit were punished with a beating. The reason for the introduction of this rule was that it was believed that smoking would prevent the boys from catching the Plague, which was raging at the time.

The first school match

Matches between schools were not played until the end of the eighteenth century. Before then football and cricket matches were always internal affairs but, with the improvement of roads at that time, matches between schools became a possibility. The first Eton v. Harrow cricket match at Lords took place in 1805. From then onwards, with the coming of the railways, interschool matches became increasingly common.

The first gym slip

The first gym slip was worn by Anna Pagan in 1892 at Madame Osterberg's Physical Training College in London. It was designed by a fellow student. The gym slip, which became the uniform of most schoolgirls up to the end of the Second World War, was important because it enabled girls to take part in sports wearing appropriate clothing. Before then long skirts had been worn, which not only hampered the players' progress but allowed for cheating in such games as hockey – when the player could gracefully stoop down and trap the ball in the folds of her skirt! To begin with, the gym slip was always worn under a long skirt except when the girls were in the gym or on the playing fields.

The first schoolboys to carry weapons

We know that the schoolboys of Eton were allowed to carry weapons because the original fifteenth-century rule book of the school said that the boys were not to carry their weapons unless walking in the town. French schoolboys were also armed at this time. The regulations of one school pointed out that firearms and swords were not to be taken into the pupils' rooms and should be left with the principal for safe keeping.

The first schoolboy mutiny

In the late eighteenth and early nineteenth centuries conditions at most schools were spartan and boys were severely beaten for trivial offences. At this time there were several schoolboy mutinies. In fact George III whenever he met boys from Eton used to ask, 'Have you had any mutinies lately, eh, eh?' In 1768 the Etonians joined the assistant masters in a battle against the headmaster. The boys broke the school windows, tore up the headmaster's papers and set fire to the block at which boys were beaten. After two days, the rebellion was quelled and the boys went home for a while to calm down.

There were rebellions at other schools too. At Winchester in 1793 the boys tore up the paving stones in the courtyard and carried them upstairs in order to defend themselves against the masters. In 1794 at Rugby a mutiny began when a boy fired a pistol out of a window. There was a mutiny over the appointment of a new head at Harrow in 1805 in which Lord Byron the poet took part. At Westminster in 1818 troops were called in to suppress a mutiny. It was thought at the time that these rebellions were in imitation of the French Revolution and were influenced by the ideas and philosophies that led up to it. The last of the school rebellions was at Marlborough in 1851; it began with forbidden fireworks and gunpowder on November 5th and ended, after a week, with the headmaster giving in to all the boys' demands!

The first rebellion against the cane

The first children to rebel against the use of the cane in schools were a crowd of schoolboys who marched to Parliament in 1699 and presented a petition to the Speaker of the House demanding that the severities of discipline in the nation's schools should cease. Their petition had no effect and the leaders of the rebellion were sent back to their schools to be caned.

The first French schoolboy mutiny

The first recorded schoolboy mutiny in France was at the Jesuit college of La Flêche in 1646. The magistrate had forbidden the customary election of a schoolboy to be King of Youth and to lead the riotous pre-Lenten carnival and some of the boys of the school had been publicly flogged. This made the boys so angry that they surrounded the school armed with swords and staves and picketed the building to prevent other scholars entering. A pitched battle then took place between the boys and the masters, who were armed with muskets and halberds. The fighting did not stop until one of the masters had received a severe injury.

The youngest teachers

The youngest teachers in England were the thirteen-year-old children in elementary schools in the nineteenth century who, as well as being pupils in schools, taught the younger children of the school under the pupil-teacher scheme that was introduced in 1846. Between the ages of thirteen and eighteen these children were apprentices in the teaching profession. This apprenticeship scheme formed the basis of the training of all elementary school teachers until 1900.

The youngest headmistress

The youngest headmistress was Hannah Wooley, born in 1623 who, when left an orphan at the age of fourteen, set up her own school. In her prospectus she offered to teach six different kinds of needlework, six different kinds of fancywork, writing and arithmetic, all manner of cooking, the making of herbal remedies and 'discerning the symptoms of most diseases' and 'several things too tedious here to relate'. She kept her school for three years until she had an offer to become a resident governess in a private house. All this experience must have been very useful to her when later she married a schoolmaster and they opened a boys' school in Hackney.

The youngest evening school instructor

The youngest evening school instructor was John Collier, born in 1708. At thirteen he was apprenticed to a weaver but his indentures were cancelled and at fourteen he became an itinerant schoolmaster, going from village to village giving classes at night to people who had been working all day. He taught reading, writing and accounts for a small fee. He worked in this fashion until he was twenty-one when he became a regular schoolmaster.

The youngest university students

In the fifteenth and sixteenth centuries people went to university much earlier than they do today. John Donne, the famous poet who was born in 1573, went to Oxford when he was only ten years old. One nineteenth-century young entrant to university was Lord Kelvin, the moving spirit in the laying of the trans-Atlantic cable, who went to Glasgow university when he was only eleven years old. Partly as a result of his long education Lord Kelvin was entitled to more letters after his name than any other man of his time. They were P.C., O.M., G.C.O., M.A., LL.D., D.C.L., D.Sc., M.D., F.R.S., F.R.S.E., D.L.

The cleverest children

The youngest person with an IQ of over 150, which is classified as representing genius, is Kim Ung-Yong, who was born in South Korea in 1963 and whose IQ at five was recorded as an amazing 210, the highest IQ ever recorded. At the age of four and a half, he already spoke four languages – Korean, English, German and Japanese – and he was able to perform integral calculus. Both his parents were university professors and he used to attend and absorb university classes with them before he had reached the normal age for attending school!

Intelligence Quotient tests were not developed

until 1905 but there are many instances of children of outstanding intelligence before this date. John Stuart Mill, the Victorian philosopher, began to learn Ancient Greek when he was three. The son of the diarist John Evelyn could read English, French and Latin at the age of two and a half and by the time he was four he understood some of the propositions of Euclid and had developed a passion for Greek. Unfortunately this early learning was not to benefit him in later life as he died at the age of five. The writers Jonathan Swift and Samuel Taylor Coleridge could both read any chapter in the Bible by the age of three. There are many more instances of remarkable learning by children of so young an age but in many cases very early teaching probably has as much to do with it as exceptional braininess.

The first 'calculating boy'

The first 'calculating boy' (the name given to a boy who could do complicated mental arithmetic very quickly) was Jerediah Buxton, who lived in the eighteenth century. He could do sums like: 'How many barleycorns would it take to stretch eight miles?' in 90 seconds. When his father took him to the theatre to see Shakespeare's *Richard III*, the boy spent his time counting the number of words spoken by David Garrick in the principal role.

A more famous mental arithmetician was George Parker Bidder of Devon (1806–78), who was known as 'the calculating phenomenon'. When he was six years old and had not long been at the village school, his father noticed how quickly and cleverly he did sums and decided to take him round the country exhibiting his powers. He was taken to Windsor

Castle to perform for Queen Charlotte, who asked him to calculate how long a snail creeping at the rate of 8 feet a day would take to travel from Land's End in Cornwall to Faraid Head in Scotland, a distance of 838 miles. He quite quickly answered, '553,080 days.'

His education was sponsored by Edinburgh businessmen and he grew up to work with George Stephenson on the railway, to found the Electric Telegraph Company and to construct the Victoria Docks in London. His son and grandson inherited excellent powers of calculation but were not as famous as George Parker Bidder.

The first 'calculating boy' in America was Zerah Colbourn, who was born in Vermont in 1804. He was brought to England when he was eight and astonished people by doing complicated sums in his head. He was sent to Westminster School by the Earl of Bristol but left when he was fifteen. As he grew older, his mathematical powers declined. Eventually Colbourn had only average ability and became a school teacher.

2
Children at war

The youngest army officer

The youngest officer in the British Army was Ensign Henry Ellis who was made an officer in the army on the day he was born in 1783. From the seventeenth to the nineteenth century officer's commissions in the army were purchased for children so that they could draw pay and so that by the time they took up the job full-time they would have been promoted to a good position! All did not run smoothly in Ensign Ellis' army career: shortly after he was commissioned his regiment was disbanded and young Henry was put on half-pay. His father soon helped him out and by the time he was five he was enlisted with another regiment. By the age of thirteen he had a captaincy in the 23rd Fusiliers. He served in the army all his life and was killed at Waterloo in 1815 when, as Colonel Sir Henry Ellis, he was leading his troops into battle.

The youngest member of a cavalry charge

The youngest person recorded as having taken part in a cavalry charge is Cornet John Floyd of Eliott's

Light Horse. In 1760 at the age of twelve he charged the French lines at Emsdorf five times. At one point his horse was shot from under him and he only escaped death at the hands of a French dragoon through the daring help of a brother-officer. After these experiences, he felt the need to get away from the hurly-burly of the battlefield and took two years' leave of absence on half-pay to complete his education. Later he became the first commander of the British cavalry in India.

The longest-serving officer in the army

Field-Marshal Sir William Gomm joined the army as an ensign in 1794 when he was ten and did not leave for the next eighty-one years.

The youngest commander in war

The youngest person to command a division in time of war was Edward of Woodstock, the Black Prince. The son of Edward III of England he led a division against the French at the Battle of Crécy in 1346 when he was only sixteen. It was a resounding victory for the English even though they were outnumbered by the French. At one stage it seemed as if the Prince and his men would be overwhelmed and the King was asked to send reserves to help his hard-pressed son.

'Is my son dead or hurt?' the King asked.

'No, sire, but he is hard beset,' came the reply.

'Then return to those who sent you and bid them send me no more messages while my son is alive; tell them to let the boy win his spurs.'

The Prince rallied his troops and soon after the battle was won.

It was after Crécy that the Black Prince (who was the second Prince of Wales) took as his device the ostrich feathers and the motto 'Ich Dien' (I serve) that had been borne by the blind King of Bohemia, who died in the battle. Every Prince of Wales has used these as his badge and motto ever since.

The youngest Victoria Cross

The Victoria Cross, Britain's highest award for bravery, has twice been awarded to boys. The youngest winner was Hospital Apprentice Arthur Fitzgibbon of the Indian Medical Service. When the Chinese Government refused to admit British and French envoys in 1859 and fired on them from the forts at the mouth of the River Pei-ho, a joint Anglo-French force was sent to take the forts. The young

Fitzgibbon was with the 67th Regiment and he displayed great coolness and courage under fire. While caring for the wounded, he received a severe injury himself and for his outstanding bravery and courage he received the Victoria Cross at the age of only fifteen.

The youngest posthumous Victoria Cross

During the First World War at the naval Battle of Jutland in 1916, Boy John Travers Cornwell of the light cruiser *Chester* was mortally wounded in the first few minutes of the action. Despite this he remained standing alone in a most exposed position beside his gun while all around him the rest of the gun crew lay dead or wounded. Boy Cornwell died two days later in hospital. He was awarded the VC for his bravery in this action.

The youngest army

Astoundingly, the youngest army in history was made up of children under twelve years old. It was the Children's Crusade of 1212 and it never fought a battle although its members dearly wanted to. It happened like this. One day in May of that year a twelve-year-old shepherd boy called Stephen took to Philip of France a letter addressed to the King which, he said, he had been given by Christ himself. Stephen said that Christ wanted him to go on a crusade to rescue the Holy Land from the Moslems. Although the King was not impressed, Stephen was not put off and went round the countryside preaching and calling upon children to help him in his task.

By June he had collected an army of several

thousand children, none of them over twelve years old. Most of them were peasant children but there were a few boys of noble families and a few older pilgrims and some priests. Stephen led his army southwards depending on charity for food. When they came to Marseilles, Stephen assured his followers that the sea would divide for them as the Red Sea had done in the Bible.

The miracle did not happen. Some of the children were discouraged and began the weary journey home but many stayed, expecting each morning that God would relent and produce the promised miracle. Finally two merchants of Marseilles offered to transport the army in seven ships to the Holy Land, an offer which Stephen accepted gratefully. The children departed and nothing more was heard from them for eighteen years.

Then in the year 1230 a priest arrived in France from the East – he had been one of the young priests who had accompanied Stephen's army. He said that the seven ships had been met by a squadron of Saracens from Africa to whom the merchants had sold the children. The priest said that some of them had been sold as slaves in Algeria, some in Alexandria in Egypt and some in Baghdad – where many of them were martyred for refusing to become Moslems. The priests had been luckier for they had been bought by the Governor of Egypt, who was interested in Western languages and literature and employed them as interpreters, translators and teachers. Eventually this one priest was released and allowed to return to France with the doleful news.

The youngest conscripted soldiers

The record for the youngest children to be called up for compulsory military service belongs to Equatorial Guinea. Here in 1976 the President decreed that military service was compulsory for all boys between the ages of seven and fourteen. Any parent refusing to allow their child to join the army would be imprisoned or shot.

The youngest pilot

The youngest known record for a qualified pilot in the British armed forces belongs to Sergeant Thomas Dobney. By lying about his age, he managed to join the RAF during the Second World War at the age of fourteen. Thus he was able to qualify as a pilot when he was only fifteen years old.

The youngest sailor

In past centuries the Royal Navy recruited sailors at a very early age but there is no official record of who was the youngest sailor. At one time in the seventeenth century the average age of officers joining the service was twelve and a half. In the eighteenth century orphan boys over the age of twelve were adopted by the Marine Society, who fitted them out and sent them to sea as apprentices. Many of the most famous admirals joined at a very young age: Nelson at twelve, Rodney at twelve, Keppel at ten, Fisher at thirteen, Jellicoe at twelve and Mountbatten at twelve.

In the early days of the navy the midshipmen had to study hard and put up with crowded conditions and bad food but they still had time to enjoy themselves. They played follow-my-leader up and down the rigging, fought mock battles on deck with brooms and even practised dancing on the quarterdeck. One lad, Edward Pellew, distinguished himself by standing on his head on the yard-arm when the ship was decked with flags in honour of a visiting general – a few days later he dived into the sea from the top of the rigging to rescue a sailor who had fallen overboard.

The youngest soldier

The youngest known soldier in the ranks was William Frederick Price, who was enlisted in the British Army on 23 May 1903 when he was eleven years old.

The youngest soldier in the American Civil War

John Lincoln Clem is thought to have been the youngest soldier to fight in the American Civil War and also the youngest soldier to wear uniform in America. At the age of nine he was refused admission to the army but despite this initial setback he managed to join a regiment unofficially and became the drummer boy for a company of soldiers. As he was not officially on the payroll the men of the regiment clubbed together to give him a small monthly salary.

The youngest boy to lose a leg in battle

In 1794 Midshipman Boys, a pupil at Dr Barrow's School in London, left to join the *Queen Charlotte* for the sea battle of the Glorious First of June. In the course of the battle Boys lost a leg. He had a wooden

leg fitted and returned to school to finish his education. A fellow pupil wrote, 'You may suppose how all the boys stared when he stumped into school with his wooden leg for he was so short a time absent he was scarcely missed.' When he had completed his schooling he went back to the navy and finished his service as a post-captain.

The first prince to go to sea

The first prince to go to sea as a midshipman was Prince William (later William IV), who joined the flagship *Prince George* when he was thirteen. His father, George III, said that he wanted the boy to have no special privileges and the Prince announced he did not wish to be known as Prince William Henry but as plain William Guelph. He was present at the battle of Cape St Vincent when he was fourteen. One of his instructors while he was still a midshipman was Nelson, who at that time was a captain in his twenties. When William came to the throne, he was always known as the 'Sailor King'.

The youngest duellist

The youngest recorded fighter of a duel is Ensign John Savage of the Forty-Eighth Foot Regiment, who fought a duel with his colonel at the age of fifteen. Savage had been an ensign since he was two years old and he finished his career as Colonel Sir John Boscawen Savage of the Royal Marines.

The youngest adjutant

The youngest adjutant in the British army was James Wolfe who died as a thirty-year-old General while taking Quebec in 1759. He was adjutant of his regiment at sixteen.

The youngest leader of a military parade

Six-year-old Stuart Gilfillan, son of the Royal Scots Dragoon Guards' drummer, became the youngest recorded person to lead a military parade when he led the regimental band on parade at Sennelager in Germany in June 1980.

3
Children in government

The youngest MPs

Everybody knows that the Members of Parliament sometimes behave like schoolboys but it is not so widely known that at one time a schoolboy could sit in

the House of Commons. It was not until 1695 that a law was passed ruling that no one under the age of twenty-one could be a Member of Parliament. Before that date children could and did take up seats in the Commons and the youngest among them were Henry Long, who was returned to Parliament by Old Sarum in 1453 when he was only fifteen, and Edmund Waller, who was also fifteen when he was elected to represent Amersham, Buckinghamshire, in 1621.

The youngest king of England

It would be nice to report that the youngest king of England was also the wisest but this is not the case. In 1442 when Henry V, the great conqueror of Agincourt, died his only son Henry became king. He was nine months old. And, as if this was not enough of an achievement for a baby, a month later young Henry's grandfather Charles VI of France died and Henry was proclaimed king of France as well. Thus at the tender age of ten months he was king of two of the most powerful nations of the world – but it was all downhill for Henry from then on.

The wars between England and France continued during the early part of his reign and with the great soldier-king Henry V now dead, the tide turned against the English. Henry never actually ruled France and in England, even when he came of age, he was too weak a character to exert any control over the noblemen of his court. The country fell into civil war.

Henry, who reigned for nearly fifty years, is generally regarded as having been simple but he was a very pious man, but when Henry VII suggested to the Pope years after the King's death that Henry might be made a saint, the Pope is reported to have replied that he must distinguish between saints and imbeciles. Henry VI was interested in education and founded the school at Eton and King's College Cambridge.

The youngest ruler of Scotland

Scotland's youngest monarch was Mary Queen of Scots, who became queen in 1542 when she was only a week old, after the death of her father James V in battle. At the age of six she was sent to France to marry the son of Henri II who was a weak and sickly boy. In 1558 Mary laid claim to the English throne and in 1559, when her husband was seventeen, she became queen of France. Her husband only lived to be king for a year and after his death she returned to Scotland. From there she was eventually driven out by a rising of the noblemen against her and fled to England and the mercy of her cousin Elizabeth I. Elizabeth saw Mary as too great a threat to her kingdom to allow her to live and, after Mary had been imprisoned for many years and despite Elizabeth's reluctance to kill an anointed queen, Elizabeth had Mary beheaded at Fotheringay Castle in 1587.

The youngest wife of a king

England's youngest queen by marriage was Queen Isabella, second wife of Richard II. When Richard's first wife Anne of Bohemia died, the King was so stricken with grief he ordered that the Palace of Shene where she died be burned to the ground. Later, for reasons of state he married Isabella of Valois, daughter of Charles VI of France, when she was only eight years old. She was considered too young to attend her own wedding feast so after the ceremony Richard kissed her, put her in a litter and handed her over to the English ladies.

Richard was extremely fond of his young wife and treated her as the daughter he never had. He installed her at Windsor Castle and appointed a huge retinue of governesses and tutors to look after her. He visited her frequently and could often be found playing with her. Isabella adored Richard. She understood nothing of the politics of his reign and when Richard was deposed she fell into the hands of Bolingbroke, who was to become Henry IV. Isabella refused to acknowledge the new king and tore his livery badges off her servants' clothes to have them replaced by those of her husband. Eventually, after her husband's murder, Isabella returned to France where she was married to the Duke of Orleans. She died at the age of twenty-one while giving birth to a baby girl.

The youngest king of France

Jean I of France must surely be the youngest king of all time for the crown became his while he was still in the womb in 1316. However, because of the French laws of male succession, had he been a girl the crown would not have been his on his birth. Despite his early advantage his reign must be one of the shortest in history because he died five days after his birth.

The youngest pretender to the throne of England

Lambert Simnel, born in 1475, was the youngest pretender to the English throne. Lambert bore a striking resemblance to the princes who were murdered in the Tower and Yorkist supporters put him up as a contender for the throne. At the age of eleven Lambert was taken to Ireland by his supporters and was crowned in Dublin Cathedral as Edward VI. He led an army to England and was defeated by Henry VII at Stoke-on-Trent in 1487. Henry VII, to his credit, did not treat young Lambert harshly after his capture. Lambert was made a scullion, or kitchen boy, in the royal service and rose from this position eventually to become the King's falconer. He died in 1525 aged fifty.

The youngest state prisoner to be executed

The youngest state prisoner to be executed was Lady Jane Grey, the nine-days' queen. In 1553, a faction who did not want Mary, Henry VIII's rightful heir, to be queen put Lady Jane Grey on the throne. On hearing the news the young girl fainted to the floor, but for nine days from 9 July to 19 July 1553 she was Queen Jane and lived in the Tower in royal state. However, her creation as queen was not a popular move. Her supporters were soon overcome and Mary, the rightful queen, took the crown.

Jane remained a prisoner in the Tower for the rest of her life. Her sixteenth birthday was spent there and in February 1554 she was beheaded. Because she was of royal blood, her execution took place on Tower Green within the walls of the Tower.

The youngest leader of a rebellion

By a strange twist of fate, the youngest leader of a national rebellion was a king of England – Richard

II. In 1381, when Richard was fourteen, an army of peasants marched on London demanding more freedom and lower taxes. Richard and a few loyal supporters rode out to meet the rebels and try to persuade them to turn back. During an argument with the King, the Lord Mayor was attacked by the leader of the rebellion, Wat Tyler, who was in turn killed. It was an ugly moment but the young King boldly averted disaster by calling to the rebels 'Let me be your leader, follow me!' So saying, he led the rebels away from London where he made them certain promises and then they dispersed. These promises were not kept but Richard had shown considerable bravery and skill at so young an age when his statesmen could see no way to avert disaster.

The youngest Prince of Wales

The eldest son of the monarch does not automatically become prince of Wales. It is a title that is conferred on him. Twenty-one princes have borne the title but they have not all become king. The title was created by Edward I when he was fighting to make Wales part of England. When Llewellyn, the last native prince of Wales, died in 1284, Edward offered the Welsh a prince who was born in their country and could speak neither English nor French. They agreed eagerly and Edward produced his baby son, who had been born at Caernarvon during the campaign and was too young to speak any language. He grew up to be Edward II.

The youngest prince to be created prince of Wales was James, the son of James II and known to history as the Old Pretender. He was made prince of Wales at his baptism when he was only a few days old.

Prince George, later George IV, was five days old when he was made prince of Wales and Albert Edward, son of Queen Victoria was twenty-nine days old when he was made prince of Wales. Albert Edward held the title longest, remaining prince of Wales for sixty years before he became King!

The youngest princess to be betrothed

The youngest English princess to be betrothed was Princess Eleanor, daughter of Edward I. When she was only four days old her father entered her into the marriage market, opening negotiations with the son of the Count of Burgundy. However, his endeavours were wasted because Eleanor died before she was five and never married.

The youngest knights

The youngest person ever knighted in England was Prince Albert Edward in 1841. At only twenty-nine days old he was made a Knight of the Garter. But he did not attend the ceremony. The youngest person to be knighted at a ceremony was Prince Richard Duke of York, the second son of Edward IV. He was only two years old when he was invested as a Knight of the Garter and his marriage followed soon after! At the early age of four he was married to Lady Anne Mowbray, who was more mature in years than him by one. She was five.

The youngest earl

The 9th Earl of Chichester inherited his father's title immediately upon birth in 1944, his father having died two months before his son came into the world.

The youngest person to be made a peer

Prince George, later George IV, was the youngest person to be made a peer of the realm. In 1762, the year he was born, he was made Earl of Chester.

Shortest-held title

The child to hold a title for the shortest length of time is believed to be Charles Brandon, 3rd Duke of Suffolk, who became duke when he was aged twelve in 1551 and lived only thirty minutes after inheriting the title. He and his elder brother had both been ill with measles, which was a dangerous disease in those days, and Charles only lived half an hour longer than his elder brother.

4
Children in the church

The youngest pope

In the middle ages church honours as well as those in government could be bought for children at a very early age. The youngest pope was only eleven years

old. He was Count Theophylact of Tusculum, who became pope as Benedict IX in 1032 after his father had purchased the dignity for him. Sad to relate for supporters of eleven-year-olds, he was a very bad pope and wasted the large income of the Papal States. He was pope for twelve-years but persistent squabbles marked this period and he was deposed and regained the papal throne once during this time.

The youngest cardinal

The youngest cardinal was Luis Antonio de Bourbon who was born in 1727 and was made a cardinal when he was only eight years old. Another young cardinal was Giovanni de Medici, who received the honour in 1489 when he was thirteen years old. Both these appointments were purchased by family money. Giovanni, after his early start eventually became Pope Leo X. Although he was already a cardinal he did not become an ordained priest or consecrated bishop until his election to the papacy.

The youngest archbishop

Hugnes, son of the Comte of Vermandois, was the youngest archbishop. Living in the tenth century, his father bought the Archbishopric of Rheims for him when he was only three years old.

The youngest bishop

The youngest bishop was Prince Frederick, Duke of York, second son of George III. He was made Bishop of Osnabruck through the influence of his father in 1764, when he was only six months old. Although he took up a military career and was a noted dandy and ladies' man in later life, he held the post of Bishop of Osnabruck for thirty-nine years.

The youngest vicars

In the fourteenth century students were given posts as vicars along with leave of absence for up to seven years to study at the universities. Thus there are many records of vicars aged fourteen, fifteen and sixteen but these boys were not delivering regular sermons in their parishes.

The youngest saint

Certainly one of the youngest, and probably the very youngest saint canonised by the church is Saint Agnes, who died around the year AD 304. She was a young Roman girl who had been brought up a Christian. Her father wanted her to marry when she was twelve but she refused, saying she did not want to belong to any man, but only to Christ. At the time Christians were being martyred in Rome and, rather than be forced to marry, Agnes offered herself as a martyr. She was executed by stabbing in the throat. Her feast day is 21 January and her emblem is the lamb.

5
Children outside the law

The youngest outlaw

The youngest of the outlaws of the 'Wild West' in America was William H. Bonney, more often known as Billy the Kid. He was born in a New York slum in 1859 but when he was three he went out west with his parents to Coffeyville, Kansas. Soon after this his father died and he and his mother moved to Silver City, New Mexico. Billy had no education for there were no schools in the frontier territories and he spent his childhood roaming the streets. At the age of twelve he killed a man in a fight by stabbing him to death for insulting his mother. Billy then ran away from Silver City and lived out on the prairie.

It is hard to tell the fact from the fiction in Billy's story but, according to legend, in the next two years he killed fifteen men. At the age of twenty-one he was sentenced to death for murder but he escaped from jail. A few weeks later he was ambushed and killed by Sheriff Pat Garrett, one of the famous lawmen of the old West.

The youngest highwayman

The youngest highwayman was William Page, who lived in the eighteenth century. As a boy, he was personal servant to an army officer, in which job he acquired a taste for fine clothes and good living. One day when he was sixteen he borrowed a pair of pistols and hired a horse and held up the Highgate coach. With the money from this robbery he started his life of crime. He and an accomplice committed over 300 hold-ups in three years. He was finally brought to justice by Henry Fielding, the magistrate who started the Bow Street Runners (the forerunners of the Metropolitan Police). He nearly escaped the rope for he was tried three times before he was eventually convicted and hanged in 1758.

The youngest smuggler

Children have probably often been involved in the smuggling activities of their parents but the youngest smuggler on record is the nine-year-old niece of a general in the American Civil War. In 1865 civilians could pass easily between the areas held by the opposing armies of North and South but adults were carefully searched to see that they were not carrying anything of use to the armies. The Southern troops were desperately short of medicines and the girl, who passed through the lines without a search, carried vital supplies of the medicines quinine and calomel in her doll's hollow head.

The youngest forger

The youngest forger is believed to be the poet Thomas Chatterton born in 1752. Young Thomas was a great devourer of books and would shut himself up in the attic of his house to read. In particular he loved old books with ornate capital letters and designs. He hated the disciplines of school but by the time he was eight he had become a great expert on medieval literature. He drew heraldic devices and pictures of knights and when he found old parchments in the attic he began to write poems in Old English. By the age of ten he was writing poems of great originality and by the age of twelve he was producing manuscripts that he declared he had discovered and had been written by a fifteenth-century Bristol priest called Thomas Rowley.

Many experts were convinced these manuscripts were a real discovery but the young forger was eventually exposed by Horace Walpole, to whom Thomas had sent some of the manuscripts. Sadly, for all his talents Chatterton found it impossible to make a living for himself either as a poet or a forger. At the ripe old age of seventeen he took arsenic and killed himself. His contemporaries always called him 'the marvellous boy' and there is a picture called 'The

Death of Chatterton' by H. Wallis in the Tate Gallery, London.

The youngest spy

In 1940 Winston Churchill recruited a sixteen-year-old boy as a spy and sent him to find out information from influential friends in Belgium. The boy was code-named Christopher Robin and Churchill used the code-name Tigger. Having got the information Christopher Robin was then to slip through enemy lines and deliver it to Lord Gort, head of the British Expeditionary Force. Christopher Robin continued to work for British Intelligence until after the end of the Second World War.

The youngest prison escaper

Jack Sheppard, who was born in 1702 and died when he was twenty-two, had a phenomenal record of escapes from prison. He worked with two thieves, Blueskin and Edgworth Bess, and together they thieved and picked pockets from their early teens. He was first caught and imprisoned when he was fifteen. He was incarcerated in a cell on the second floor of St Giles Roundhouse. With the aid of a razor he cut a hole in the wooden roof, wriggled through and let himself down to freedom with a rope made from strips of bed linen.

The next time he was caught he and Bess were put in Newgate Prison. Blueskin smuggled a file to them and Jack sawed through the manacles on his wrists and ankles and then set to work on the window bars. Jack squeezed through the hole he had cut but Bess, being fatter, had to remove her clothes before she too

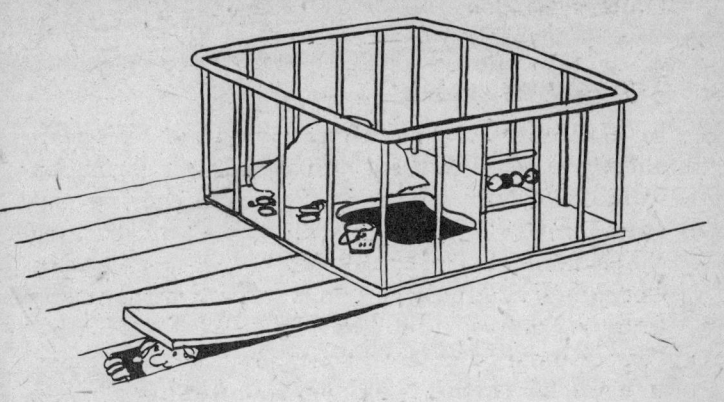

could make her way out. They then scaled a twenty-foot wall and escaped.

Jack straight away took up the profession of highway robbery and soon found himself held in Newgate again – and this time it was in the condemned man's hold. Nothing daunted, Bess smuggled a file to him and Jack again filed his way to freedom. Soon back in Newgate for the fourth time, Jack's gaolers put him on the third storey and securely chained him to the floor. Jack managed to free a nail from the floorboards and use it to undo his chains. It was then a simple matter for him to reach freedom via a chimney, a disused cell, the prison chapel and several locked doors.

Jack was not rewarded for his talents. The fifth time he was caught, a constant watch was kept on him day and night and in 1724 he was hanged at Tyburn. He was the darling of the crowds, who admired his spirit in making so many daring and difficult escapes.

Hanging and transportation

In the past the law has taken a much less lenient attitude to children than it does today. In the eighteenth century children of over seven were considered to be responsible for their crimes and therefore children over the age of seven could be hanged. For example on one day alone in February 1814 five children were condemned to death: two boys aged twelve for burglary and three aged eight, nine and eleven respectively for stealing a pair of shoes.

The alternative to hanging was transportation to the colonies. In 1894 a boy of fourteen was sentenced to transportation for stealing a silk handkerchief and a young girl of ten was transported for stealing a shawl or petticoat. It is impossible to find out who was the youngest child to be hanged but it is known that children under the age of seven were quite often hanged, either because they did not know their age or they could not prove they were under seven.

6
Children on stage and screen

The youngest actors

The youngest actors to appear regularly on the stage in England were the Children of the Chapel Royal in the reign of Elizabeth I. Their ages ranged from ten to thirteen years and they sang the services every day for the Queen. They were trained to sing, dance, play musical instruments and act and they took part in masques and plays for the Queen. The boys who were the best actors lived at Blackfriars at her expense and performed a play for her every week.

The Master of the Children of the Chapel Royal had a patent from the Queen to impress into her service any boy he thought suitable. He took boys from schools and apprenticeships for the Chapel.

The first child to appear in a film

The first child to appear in films was a fourteen-year-old boy called Duval, who worked for the Lumière brothers, the French film pioneers. The film was called *L'Arroseur Arrosé* (The Waterer Watered) and it was first shown in Paris in 1895. It was a short piece showing a gardener watering a flowerbed with a hose. Duval creeps up behind him and puts his foot on the hose to stop the water flowing. When the puzzled gardener holds up the nozzle to look down it to seek the cause of the trouble, the boy steps back and jumps about with glee as the gardener receives a faceful of water.

The first close-up film shot

The first person to appear in close-up in a British film was a little boy called Bert Massey, who appeared in a short film called *Grandma's Reading Glass* in 1900. The little boy was shown examining various things with the magnifying glass, including a newspaper and his grandmother's eye.

This came very soon after the first American close-up, a film of a man sneezing!

The first child star

The first child to be named as a star in a film was six-year-old Jackie Coogan, who was chosen by Charlie Chaplin to play the lead part in his film *The Kid* in 1920. Chaplin discovered Coogan, the son of a vaudeville artist, when he was four years old but it took him some while to find just the right story in which to introduce the boy. The film was a heart-rending story full of emotion and was a huge success. In the years that followed, Jackie Coogan starred in film after film and was extremely popular at the box office. He is still acting in films today.

The youngest star in talking pictures

Baby Le Roy, who was born in 1931, was probably the youngest actor in talking pictures. He was two when he first appeared in a film with W. C. Fields, an actor who was a notorious 'child-hater'. Fields is supposed one day to have put gin into Baby Le Roy's orange juice.

The youngest Oscar winner

Shirley Temple is the youngest person ever to receive an Oscar, the American film industry's most coveted trophy. It was a special award given 'in grateful recognition of her outstanding contribution to the screen industry'. She received it in 1934 when she was six.

The youngest Oscar for acting

The youngest person to receive an Oscar for acting is Tatum O'Neal, daughter of film star Ryan O'Neal. In 1973, when she was ten, Tatum O'Neal won the award for the best actress in a supporting role for her performance in *Paper Moon*.

The youngest nomination for an Oscar

In 1980, Justin Henry became the youngest actor to be nominated for an Academy acting award when he was put forward as best actor for his role in *Kramer vs. Kramer* at the age of eight.

The top money-earners

Each year a list is published of the names of the top money-making stars of the year. Shirley Temple was top money-making female star of the movies for five years running, from 1935 to 1939, when she was eleven years old. Mickey Rooney was top money-making man for three years running from 1939 to 1941, when he reached the age of eighteen.

The youngest film cast

The film with the youngest cast was Fox–Rank's 1976 movie *Bugsy Malone*, in which all the parts were played by children. The film was a spoof gangster movie and Jodie Foster, aged eleven, received the B.A.F.T.A. award for the best supporting actress for her performance in the film.

The youngest television cast

The television show with the youngest cast is *Doctors and Nurses*, produced by London Weekend Television. Children play all the parts in this spoof soap-opera except for one guest star who is an adult actor each week.

The youngest television writer

The youngest television playwright is Yolanda Casey, aged thirteen, whose play *Strike* won a Thames Television competition. The play was shown in March 1980. Yolanda also had a stage play, *Mrs Katy Brown Solves a Mystery*, presented as part of a festival at the Contact Theatre Manchester.

The first child in a British film

The first child to act in a British film was Ivy Millais who played the title role in *Oliver Twist*, the first British feature film, which was made at Hepworth Studios, Walton-on-Thames, in 1912. It was a sixty-minute film, which did well at the box office even though the film-maker, Hepworth, did not think it very distinguished.

The first royal children to be filmed

The first child in the royal family to be filmed was Prince Edward (later Edward VIII, and Duke of Windsor), who was filmed when he was two at Balmoral in 1896. Queen Victoria wrote in her diary, 'We were photographed by Downey by the new cinematagraphic process which makes moving pictures by winding off a reel of film. We were walking up and down and the children jumping about.' The other child in the film was the Grand Duchess Olga, daughter of the Tsar of Russia.

The first child to appear in a circus

The first child to appear in a circus was a drummer boy who provided the dramatic drum rolls that accompanied the feats of trick riding at Astley's Circus. Astley's Circus was the first circus to be set up in England and was founded in 1769 by former Sergeant-Major Astley.

The youngest clown

The youngest circus clown was Joseph Grimaldi, born in 1779, who appeared at Sadler's Wells just before his second birthday with his father, who was also a clown. In one of his early performances he narrowly escaped losing his life. Young Joe was dressed as a monkey on the end of a chain, which was whirled round his father's head; one day the chain broke and poor little Joe sailed into the audience, where he was fortunately caught in the arms of an old gentleman. Grimaldi grew up to be the most famous clown of all time.

The youngest tightrope-walker

The youngest tightrope-walker was Jean Francois Gravelet, better known as Blondin, who first appeared in a circus billed as 'The Little Wonder' aged five. In 1859 he became famous as the man who crossed Niagara Falls on a tightrope, a distance of over 1000 feet. To cap this daring act, he crossed and re-crossed, giving himself increasingly difficult handicaps: he did the crossing blindfolded, he went over on stilts, he pushed a wheelbarrow in front of

him, he hopped across in a sack, he carried a man across on his shoulders, he took a portable stove with him and cooked an omelette halfway across. He even offered to push the Prince of Wales (later Edward VIII) across in a wheelbarrow but the Prince, who enjoyed the act hugely, politely declined the offer.

The youngest 'death leap'

The youngest trapeze artist to achieve the *salto mortale*, or 'death leap', which consists of three somersaults between two trapezes, was Tom Stickney aged fourteen, who did this stunt in New York in 1931. At that time only two or three people had ever done it and several had been killed or severely injured in the attempt.

The youngest circus dwarf

The youngest dwarf to appear in a circus was an American, General Tom Thumb, whose real name was Charles Stratton. He was discovered in 1842 by the famous showman Philo T. Barnum. The ten-year-old child was less than 2 feet tall and under 16 pounds in weight. The general was exhibited for two years in America and then Barnum brought him over to England where, when he was twelve, he appeared daily at the Egyptian Hall, Piccadilly and at nights at the Lyceum Theatre, where a fairy tale, *Hop O' My Thumb*, was specially adapted for him. Queen Victoria sent for him and the general was taken to Buckingham Palace to meet the royal family, who enjoyed his antics enormously. He was very popular in London and made a great deal of money for Barnum and received many splendid presents for himself. These included a coach 20 inches high and 11 inches wide, drawn by Shetland ponies, with two little boys in pale blue livery who acted as coachman and footman.

When Tom Thumb made a return visit to London in 1857 he no longer had the same appeal – the public were not as interested in a man dwarf as they had been in a boy dwarf. He returned to America, where he retired on the money he had made earlier and married another dwarf. They had one child, who grew to normal size.

7
Children in the arts

The first child authoress

The first young author to have a book published was Daisy Ashford, who wrote *The Young Visiters, or Mr Salteena's Plan* when she was nine years old. It was published in 1919 when she was grown up, complete with the spelling mistakes that combined with the use of long words not always perfectly understood by

the authoress, make it so endearing. J. M. Barrie wrote a preface. The book received much critical acclaim and immediately went into twenty editions. It is still in print.

The youngest published English author

The youngest published author in Britain is Janet Aitchison, who wrote *The Pirates' Tale* when she was five and a half. It was published by Puffin Books in 1969, when she was six and a half.

The youngest published American author

The youngest published author in America is Dorothy Straight, born in 1958, who wrote *How the World Began* when she was four. It was published in 1964 by Pantheon Books, New York.

The youngest published diarist

The youngest child to have her diary published is Marjory Fleming who was born in 1803. To encourage Marjory to practise her handwriting, her governess had made her keep a journal and in 1858 this journal was published. Among the many sentiments expressed in the diary with which children will sympathise was a hearty dislike of mathematical tables. She wrote: 'I am now going to tell you about the horrible and wretched plague that my multiplication gives me, you can't conceive it. The most deveillish thing is 8 x 8 and 7 x 7 is what nature itself can't endure.' As the result of this published diary, Marjory became the youngest person ever to have an entry in *The Dictionary of National Biography*.

The youngest author of a best-seller

The youngest author to have a book in the best-seller lists is Sarah Patterson, who wrote *The Distant Summer* when she was fourteen. It was published by Hutchinson and, in America, by Simon and Schuster. It featured on the *Sunday Times* best-seller list for ten weeks.

The youngest painter

The youngest painter to have a picture accepted by the Royal Academy was five-year-old Lewis Lyons, who had a picture called 'Trees and Monkeys' accepted and hung in the 1967 Summer Exhibition. Before that, the record was held by Sir Edward Landseer (1802–73), Queen Victoria's favourite painter, who exhibited a picture at the Royal Academy in 1815 when he was thirteen years old.

The youngest stamp designer

The youngest people to design postage stamps are two six-year-olds, Tasveer Shemza of Stafford and James Berry of Bromley. They won the top prizes for designing Christmas stamps for the Post Office in 1966.

The youngest first-day cover designer

The youngest designer of a 'first-day cover' for the Post Office is Adrian Cresswell aged five. In 1979 the children's television programme *Blue Peter* in conjunction with the Post Office held a competition to design a first-day cover for the special stamps that were to be issued to celebrate the International Year of the Child. Adrian's winning design was decorated with a train, from each carriage of which people of all nations were waving gaily to symbolize world friendship.

The youngest composer

The youngest composer and concert pianist was Wolfgang Amadeus Mozart (1756–91), who began to play keyboard when he was two and at the age of five was already composing pieces for the clavier. When he was seven his father, who was court musician to the Archbishop of Salzburg, took young Wolfgang on a concert tour, during which he played at all the principal courts of Europe. During this trip while he was in Paris, he composed his first sonatas for violin and clavier.

When he was on an Italian tour in 1771 aged fifteen he heard the 'Miserere' of Gregorio Allegri played in the Sistine Chapel and, when he came out, he sat down and wrote out the music without a fault. By the time he died, aged thirty-five, he had composed a great many brilliant concertos and operas. Mozart also holds the record for being the fastest-known composer, probably because he composed his music in his head and then wrote it straight down without correction.

The youngest violinist

The youngest concert violinist was Yehudi Menuhin, born in 1916, who was playing solo violin concerts all over Europe, at the age of seven. He is still one of the world's most famous violinists and has done much to encourage young people with talent to take up musical careers. Like Mozart, he is an example of a child prodigy who went on to greater things as an adult. At the age of fifteen Yehudi Menuhin became the youngest person to have an entry in *Who's Who*.

Niccolò Paganini (1782–1840) was another famous violinist who gave concerts when he was very young – he gave his first recitals at Florence and Genoa at the age of nine.

A third child prodigy of the violin was Jascha Heifetz, who was born in 1901 in Russia but later became an American citizen. He studied at the St Petersburg Conservatoire and gave his first public recital at the age of nine. He is considered one of the world's finest violinists.

The youngest opera singer

The youngest person to have a major role in an opera is Jeanette Gloria La Bianca, born in 1934, of the USA. She sang Rosina in *The Barber of Seville* in Rome in 1950 when she was fifteen.

The youngest concert singer

In the eighteenth century there was a very popular singer in London who entertained at musical soirées. She was called Karolina Stenz and she was three and a half years old.

The youngest conductor

The youngest conductor is Pierino Gamba (born in 1937), from Italy. He made his début as a conductor at the age of eight and toured Europe, South America and the USA.

The youngest golden disc

The youngest recording artist to achieve sales of over a million records and qualify for a golden disc is Osamu Minagawa of Japan. He won it for his single released in 1969 when he was six years old. It was called 'Kuro Neko Tango' or 'Black Cat Tango'.

The youngest boy chart-topper

The youngest singer to top the British pop music charts was Jimmy Osmond (born in 1963) with 'Long-Haired Lover from Liverpool'. He did it in 1972 when he was nine years old.

The youngest girl chart-topper

The youngest girl to top the British pop music charts was Helen Shapiro, who had two number-one records in 1961: 'You Don't Know' in July and 'Walking Back to Happiness' in September. She was fourteen years old.

The youngest barber-shop quartet

The youngest barber-shop quartet to have a contract to sing regularly was the Osmond brothers. They were hired to sing at Disneyland in 1962 when Alan was thirteen, Wayne was eleven, Merrill was nine and Jay was seven. The following year they got a TV contract to appear for five years on the Andy Williams Show.

The Osmonds also hold the record for the family with the most members appearing on the stage together (Alan, Wayne, Merrill, Jay, Donny, Marie and Jimmy).

Jimmy, the baby of the family, was the first Osmond to win a golden disc. The record was called 'My Little Darling'.

8
Children in sport

The youngest international footballer

The world's youngest international footballer was G. Dorval, who played for Brazil against Argentina in 1957 when he was fifteen.

The youngest Scottish footballer

The youngest footballer in the Scottish League final was Derek Johnstone, who played for Rangers against Celtic in 1970 when he was sixteen.

The youngest FA cup player

The youngest player ever to take part in the FA Cup competition was Scott Endersby, who was fifteen when he played goal for Kettering against Tilbury in November 1977.

The best schoolboy player

The best achievement in international schoolboy soccer was that of Richard Smith Bell of England, who in the 1935–6 season scored twelve goals in three internationals: three against Scotland, three against Wales and six against Ireland.

The highest goal scorer

The record for the most goals scored in amateur football is held by eleven-year-old Jonathan Wright of Woodbridge, Suffolk who scored one hundred and eleven goals in the 1979–80 season.

The best header

The record for repeatedly heading a football is held by fifteen-year-old Colin Jones, who at Queensferry in 1961 headed the ball 3412 times in 34 minutes 8 seconds.

The youngest county cricket player

The youngest person to play cricket for his county was W. G. Grace (1848–1915), who first played for Gloucestershire when he was sixteen and continued to do so until he was sixty. In this time he made a total of 54,896 runs, took 2876 wickets and held 871 catches. He appeared in twenty-two Test matches and was captain of England thirteen times. He was the first cricketer to get two centuries in a match, the first to complete the double of 1000 runs and 100 wickets in a season (1873) and the first batsman to score 100 centuries in first-class cricket.

The highest individual innings

Several of the cricket records held by schoolboys excel even the achievements of first-class cricketers.

The highest-ever individual innings was scored by A. E. J. Collins when he was thirteen. He scored 628 runs not out, it took him 6 hours 30 minutes, spread over five afternoons' batting in a house match between Clarke's and Poole's houses at Clifton College, Bristol, in 1899.

The most consecutive wickets

In first-class cricket the most consecutive wickets taken by a bowler is four wickets with four consecutive balls, but two schoolboys did better. Stephen Fleming, bowling for Marlborough College 'A' XI against Bohally Intermediate at Blenheim, New Zealand in 1967, took nine consecutive wickets with nine consecutive balls. He equalled the achievement of another schoolboy, Paul Hugo, who took nine consecutive wickets with nine consecutive balls for Smithfield School against Aliwal North in South Africa in 1931.

The best wicket-keeping

The best wicket-keeping record was at Repton School where H. W. P. Middleton, keeping wicket for Priory House against Mitre House in 1930, achieved nine dismissals: eight batsmen stumped and one caught in a single innings.

The youngest Wimbledon champion

The youngest tennis champion was Lottie Dod, who won the Women's Singles at Wimbledon in 1887 aged fifteen and a half. She won the title again in 1888, 1891, 1892 and 1893.

Charlotte Dod is also remarkable because she was probably the most versatile sportswoman ever. Besides winning the Women's Singles five times, she was British Ladies' Golf Champion in 1904, she won an Olympic silver medal for archery in 1908, she represented England at hockey in 1899 and she also excelled at skating and toboganning.

The youngest quadruple tennis champion

Maureen Connolly of the USA (1935–69) was the youngest person and the first woman to hold all four major international tennis titles at the same time. She won the USA title in 1951 when she was sixteen, in 1952 she won Wimbledon and retained the USA title. In 1953 she won the French and Australian titles, won Wimbledon for the second time and the USA title for the third time. In 1954 she won her second French title and her third Wimbledon title and might have gone to take the others again but she had to give up tennis that year because she was seriously injured in a riding accident. She was very short and slight and was affectionately known to the press and her fans as 'Little Mo' or 'Mighty Mo'.

The youngest player at Wimbledon

The youngest player to take part in the Wimbledon championships is Tracey Austin of the USA (born in 1962) who was fourteen and a half in 1977 when she took part in her first tournament at Wimbledon. In 1979 she became the youngest-ever winner of the US championship, being younger than Maureen Connolly by a few months.

The youngest seeded player at Wimbledon

Andrea Jaegar of the USA became the youngest seeded player at Wimbledon at the age of fifteen years and three weeks in 1980. At fifteen, she was also the youngest player to be selected for the Wightman Cup.

The youngest gold medal for athletics

The youngest Olympic gold medallist in athletics was Barbara Jones (born in 1937) of the USA who was a member of the winning 4 × 100 metres relay team at Helsinki in 1952 when she was fifteen.

The youngest British international athletes

The youngest athletes to represent Great Britain internationally are Ross Hepburn (born in 1961), who competed against the USSR in 1977 aged fifteen, and Janis Walsh (born in 1960), who competed against Belgium in the 600 metres and 4 × 200 metre relay in 1975 aged fourteen.

The youngest world record for athletics

The youngest person to break a world record in athletics was Ulrike Meyfarth (born in 1956) of West Germany, who achieved 1.92 metres in the women's high jump, winning a gold medal in the 1972 Olympic Games at Munich when she was sixteen.

The youngest Channel swimmer

The youngest person to swim the English Channel was Markus Hooper (born in 1967) who swam from

Dover to Sangatte, France, in 14 hours 37 minutes in August 1979 aged twelve.

The youngest world record for swimming

The youngest person to break a world record for swimming was Karen Muir of South Africa (born in 1952), who broke the women's 110 yards backstroke world record in Blackpool in 1965 when she was twelve. Her time was 1 minute 8.7 seconds.

Gertrude Ederle (born in 1906) of the USA broke the women's freestyle 880 yards record in Indianapolis, USA, in 1919 when she was thirteen. Gertrude Ederle went on, when she was twenty, to become the first woman to swim the Channel, swimming from Cap Gris-Nez, France, to Dover in August 1926 in the then record time of 14 hours 39 minutes.

The first gold medal for swimming

The first people under sixteen to win Olympic gold medals for swimming were two Japanese at the 1952

Olympic Games at Los Angeles: Yasuji Miyazaki aged sixteen won the 100 metres freestyle and Kusio Kitamura aged fourteen won the 1500 metres.

The first girls' gold medal for swimming

The first girl under sixteen to win the women's 100 metres freestyle was Dawn Fraser of Australia at the Olympic Games at Melbourne in 1956. She set a world record of 62 seconds. She also won a silver medal for the 400 metres women's freestyle and was in the winning Australian 4 × 100 metres freestyle relay team.

She won the 100 metres women's freestyle again in 1960 at Rome and for a third time at Tokyo in 1964, breaking her own world record with a time of 59.5 seconds. She is the only swimmer to win the same Olympic title three times in three successive games.

At the Tokyo Games Dawn decided she would like the Japanese flag from the Emperor's palace as a souvenir. When the police discovered her taking it they gave chase but she dived into the moat and swam away. However when the Emperor heard of the escapade he was not angry but gave her the flag as a present.

The first triple gold medallist for swimming

The first person under sixteen to win three Olympic gold medals at the same games is Debbie Meyer of Sacramento, USA, who won the women's freestyle 200 metres, 400 metres and 800 metres at Mexico in 1968 when she was sixteen.

The youngest triple gold medallist for swimming

The youngest person to win three Olympic gold medals (also a silver and a bronze) at the same games was Shane Gould of Australia, who was fifteen at the 1972 Munich Games when she won and broke the world records for the women's 200 metres, 400 metres and 200 metres individual medley (freestyle, backstroke, breaststroke and butterfly). Her silver medal was for the 800 metres freestyle and her bronze was for the 100 metres freestyle. All through the games she carried a koala bear mascot to bring her luck – it certainly did the trick.

The youngest diving champion

The youngest Olympic diving champion was Marjorie Gestring of the USA, who won the springboard championship at the Berlin Olympic Games in 1936 when she was thirteen.

The youngest Olympic winner

The youngest participant in a world title event is Bernard Malvoire of France who was twelve when he coxed the winning coxed fours in the Olympic regatta at Helsinki in 1952.

The youngest British Olympic competitor

The youngest competitor to represent Great Britain in the Olympic Games was Magdalena Colledge, who was eleven when she skated in the 1932 Winter Olympics at Lake Placid.

The youngest Winter Olympic gold medal

Sonja Henie (born in 1912) of Norway was a champion skater at twelve. She went to Chamonix to take part in the Winter Olympics when she was eleven and although she had a low score there, she gained valuable experience and at twelve became Norwegian skating champion. She won her first gold medal at the Winter Olympics at St Moritz in 1928 when she was sixteen, a second at Lake Placid in 1932 and a third at Garmisch-Partenkirchen in 1936. She is the only skater to take the same title in three successive Games. She also won ten world championships. Then she turned professional and went to Hollywood, where she starred in many skating films and became a multi-millionaire.

The youngest international gymnast

The youngest international gymnast is Anita Jokiel of Poland, who competed at Brighton in 1977 two days after her eleventh birthday.

The youngest triple gold medal gymnast

Nadia Comaneci (born 1961) of Rumania was fourteen when she won three gold medals at the Olympic Games in Montreal in 1976. She achieved seven perfect scores of 10.00 at these games; this is the highest scoring ever achieved in Olympic gymnastics.

The youngest baseball player

The youngest major league baseball player was the Cincinnati pitcher J. H. Muxhall (born in 1928), who began to play professionally at the age of fifteen.

The youngest hole-in-one

The youngest golfer to have holed a ball in one is Coby Orr (born in 1970) of Colorado, USA, who when playing at San Antonio, Texas, played the fifth hole (94 metres) in one shot in 1975 when he was five years old.

The youngest table tennis international

The youngest international table tennis player and probably the youngest international in any sport is Joy Foster, who at the age of eight in 1958 was the Jamaican singles and mixed doubles champion.

The youngest chess prodigies

The youngest chess prodigy was Samuel Reshevsky, born in Poland, who at the age of eight toured Germany, Holland, England, France and the USA giving simultaneous displays against many players. His scores were usually above 90 per cent. When he was eleven he took part in a tournament against masters, scoring two wins out of five, including one victory over a grandmaster.

There have been many cases of remarkable young chess players, among them the following.

José Raoul Capablanca y Graupera (1888–1942), usually known as Capablanca, was champion of Cuba at the age of twelve.

Boris Spassky (born in 1937) of Leningrad, USSR, was Soviet candidate master at eleven and international master at sixteen.

Bobby Fischer (born in 1943) of Chicago, USA, was international master at fourteen and international grandmaster at fifteen.

Arturo Pomar was Spanish chess champion at eleven and international master at fourteen.

Elaine Saunders (now Mrs Pritchard) won an international girls' under-21 chess tournament aged twelve and became British Ladies' Champion at thirteen.

Nigel Short of Bolton (born in 1965) won the title international master in 1979 aged fourteen.

The youngest press-up record-holder

The youngest person to hold the record for the most consecutive press-ups is Chick Linster of the USA, who, aged sixteen in October 1965, did 6006 press-ups in 3 hours 54 minutes.

The youngest hula hoop record-holder

The record for keeping the most hula hoops in motion at once is 62 hoops; it is held by Jo Ann Barnes of California, USA, who was aged fifteen when she set this record and became co-winner of the USA National Hula Hoop Contest in 1976.

9
Odds and ends

The youngest hotel inspector

The youngest hotel inspector for *The Good Food Guide* is Catherine Wright who carried out inspections when she was only sixteen. She was still at school at the time and carried out her inspections of restaurants in her free time.

The youngest roller skating coach

The youngest roller skating coach in Great Britain is Karen Anglis who coached in Tottenham at the age of twelve. She teaches roller skating sixteen hours a week in addition to doing her school work and practising her own roller skating. After only skating a year, she was already a member of the Federation of Roller Skating Coaches.

The youngest sharp-shooter

The youngest champion sharpshooter in the old West was Annie Oakley. Born Phoebe Anne Oakley Mozee in 1859, she learned to shoot with a muzzle loader as a child in the backwoods of Ohio. While she was still in her teens she took part in an all-comers challenge match in marksmanship at Cincinnati, beating Frank Butler, the best marksman of the day. Butler was not only impressed with her shooting: he fell in love with her and married her. Together they went into Buffalo Bill's Wild West Show where she was billed as 'Little Sure Shot' and performed amazing feats with the rifle. The show toured Europe and she once shot the ash off a cigarette held in the mouth of Kaiser Wilhelm of Germany. Her exploits have long been remembered and in the 1940s a musical play and film were made about her called *Annie Get Your Gun*.

The youngest motorbike stunt rider

The youngest motorbike stunt rider is Darius Goodwin aged six who weighed only two and a half stone. He can ride through a brick wall, along a narrow plank and under a pole only three-quarters of an inch

higher than his handlebars. He can also ride downstairs and through a burning hoop. He demonstrated his ability to jump with his motorbike on television in *Thames News* in February 1980 when he jumped over his father who had very trustingly lain down for him. His father is a professional stunt rider and he has helped Darius who has been riding motorbikes since he was three. Darius has five special bikes and often performs before large crowds, although he is of course not allowed on the public highway.

The first motor-tourists

The drivers of the first car to make a tour were Eugen and Richard Benz aged fifteen and thirteen. They were also probably the youngest drivers on the public highway. When the motor car was first invented there was no law about the age you had to have reached in order to drive and it was not until 1930 in England that a minimum age of seventeen was introduced. Eugen and Richard's father was the inventor of the Benz car. He had taught his children to drive but had forbidden them to do it without his super-

vision. But in 1888 their mother wanted to visit relatives at Pforzheim which was 180 kilometres from Mannheim where the family lived. The three of them took the car out without Herr Benz's permission.

Eugen and Richard took turns to drive and they had several mishaps on the way. The leather linings on the brakes wore out and they had to stop to replace the leather. The fuel pipe blocked and Frau Benz cleared it with her hat pin and several other minor faults developed all of which they sorted out with great ingenuity. When they returned home at the end of the visit, the boys persuaded their father to add another gear to the engine – they said they had done enough car-pushing up hills to last a lifetime.

The youngest round-the-world sailors

The youngest round-the-world sailors are Eve and Jimmy Swale. The Swale parents and Eve left Southampton in their catamaran *Anna Liese* in 1970 when Eve was eighteen months old. On Eve's second birthday Jimmy was born on board. The family then continued on their voyage: from Gibralter they sailed to Barbados, through the Panama Canal to Australia and New Zealand and then round Cape Horn and back to England again. Eve and Jimmy are also probably the youngest sailors to round Cape Horn, something that Sir Francis Chichester said that it would be madness to do without a professional crew. The 26,000 mile voyage in the thirty foot catamaran took three years.

The youngest Titanic survivor

Everyone knows that the great ship the *Titanic* sank on 14 April 1912 on her maiden voyage when she collided with an iceberg. Nearly 2000 passengers were drowned but some survived. The youngest survivor was eleven-month-old Travers Allison, son of a Montreal banker, who was carried safely to a lifeboat by a nurse. His father, mother and three-year-old sister Lorraine all went down with the ship.

The youngest Pilgrim Father

In 1620 a band of Puritans left England in the little ship Mayflower to found a colony in America where they would have freedom to follow their religion as they wished. While the *Mayflower* was at sea, one of the passengers, Elizabeth Hopkins, gave birth to her fourth child who was christened Oceanus. When the little band, who were to become the founding fathers of America, landed at Plymouth Rock, Oceanus Hopkins was still only a few weeks old.

The youngest millionaire

The youngest millionaire was Shirley Temple who earned over one million dollars as a film star before she was ten years old.

The youngest self-made businessman

The youngest person to start his own business and turn it into a world-famous, multi-million pound concern was William R. Morris born in 1877. When he was fourteen, he walked out of his first job in a bicycle repair shop and set up with a capital of £4 to do the work on his own. At first he worked from his father's garden shed but he was soon able to open a shop in Oxford High Street. He began to build bicycles as well as to repair them. He rode his own bicycles in races and became a champion which increased the demand. Soon he was employing five men and a boy.

He was fascinated by motor cars which were just appearing but he could not afford to produce them so he built extra strong bicycles instead and fitted them with engines to make the first motorbikes. He then set to work to build his own model of car which he launched at the Motor Show in 1912 and called the Morris Oxford. He took enough orders for it to go into production in a workshop at Cowley. He made a great deal of money from this car and much of it he used to help other people giving money in particular to medical research, hospitals and universities.

The youngest inventor

The youngest recorded inventor is Christopher Wren who was born in 1632 and is most famous as architect of St Paul's Cathedral in London. When he was fourteen he invented an instrument for use in astronomy which he dedicated to his father in Latin verse. He then set to work to invent a pneumatic machine.

Another young inventor was Walter Lines who invented the scooter in 1897 when he was fifteen. Unfortunately he did not patent the invention, so it was soon copied and he made very little money from it. However when he grew up he invented the fairy cycle and founded the well-known toymaking firm Triang toys.

The youngest workers

The youngest children in England to do a full day's work for pay were the children of poor families in the eighteenth and nineteenth centuries. The youngest of these were the climbing boys who worked for chimney sweeps and were often set to work at three years old. Their job was to go up chimneys and dislodge the soot, a job that could only be performed by a very small child. The children suffered terribly and Charles Kingsley in particular drew attention to their plight in his book *The Water Babies*. However it was not until 1875 that a law was passed making it illegal to send children up chimneys.

The youngest merchant adventurer

The youngest merchant adventurer was Marco Polo who was born in 1254. His father and uncle were both Venetian merchants who were on a trading mission to the court of Kublai Khan in China when Marco was born. They returned to Venice several years later and on their second journey took him with them when he was only fifteen. The journey took them four years and they travelled through Mesopotamia, down the Persian Gulf and across the mountains and deserts of Central Asia to Peking.

The youngest explorer

The youngest explorer was John Stewart born in 1749. His parents and teachers despaired of him in his early years. He was expelled from a local school at the age of six, and from Harrow, where he refused to do any work, at ten. He was then sent to Charterhouse where he would not do any lessons except English. So by the age of fourteen his father despaired of his getting an education and sent him to India to work as a clerk with the East India Company in Madras. Stewart was shocked at the corruption he found, and soon resigned to start to explore India on foot. At the age of sixteen he set off into the almost unknown interior of India. He then joined Hyder Ali's army and quickly rose to the rank of General but was invalided out with a head wound. He left Mysore and walked to Arcot where he took a post as Prime Minister to an Indian Prince or Nabob. In this position Stewart managed to save £3,000 for himself and he lived on the income of this money for the rest of his life, the rest of which he spent walking and exploring until his death at seventy-three. He was always known as 'Walking Stewart'.

The youngest marrieds

Before 1929 when the age of consent to marriage was set at sixteen, very young children from rich families were often married in order to join properties together or to make settlements which would increase the wealth of their families. Two of the youngest known married couples were John Somerford aged three and Jane Bereton aged two who were carried into church in their parent's arms in 1564 and Robert Parre aged two and Elizabeth Rogerson aged two who married in the same year. It is reported that Robert had to be bribed by his uncle with an apple to get him to go into the church.

The youngest three-times married

The only recorded person to marry three times before the age of twelve was Grace de Saleby, a fifteenth century heiress. At four she was married to a nobleman who soon died. At six she remarried and was again quickly widowed. When she was eleven she married for a third time to another nobleman who paid the price of three hundred marks for the privilege.

The youngest appeal under the Sex Discrimination Act

The youngest person to appeal under the Sex Discrimination Act, which says that men and women must be treated equally, was Teresa Bennett aged twelve. Her local county court ruled that the ban imposed to stop her playing football for a boy's team was illegal under the act. However, the Football Association appealed against the decision and won the case so that Teresa was not allowed to play football with the boy's team after all.

The youngest sword-wearer

The youngest child to appear in public wearing a sword was the Dauphin Louis of France. Born in 1601, the young Louis wore a sword strapped to his side at the age of one when he greeted the Venetian ambassador. A satin shirt was put over the swaddling bands in which he was customarily dressed, a military hat was put on his head and to complete the costume he wore boots and spurs on his feet. He may also be the youngest person to hold a diplomatic audience with an ambassador.

The youngest prisoner in the Tower

Prince Richard, son of Edward IV, was the youngest prisoner held in the Tower of London. He was eleven years old when he joined his brother Edward V there soon after his father's death on the orders of his uncle, Richard Duke of Gloucester. At first it was said that the princes were in the Tower for safekeeping before Edward's coronation but the coronation was repeatedly postponed and eventually their parent's marriage was declared invalid and their uncle was proclaimed King as Richard III. The Princes were never seen alive again after 1483. It will never be known who murdered them but suspicion falls most heavily on their uncle Richard III. At the time there were many rumours about their deaths and a chronicler wrote 'Some said they were murdered atween two feather beds, some said they were drowned in malvesey (wine) and some said they were sticked with a venomous potion.' In 1674, workmen digging under a staircase in the White Tower found the skeleton's of two children. Modern medical evidence suggests that these were indeed the bones of the Princes and that they probably died from suffocation. The bones were transferred to Westminster Abbey where they still are today.

The first Barnado boy

The first Barnado boy was ten-year-old Jim Jarvis. Thomas Barnado (1845–1905) was a young Irishman who wanted to go to China as a medical missionary but when he came to England to study at the London Hospital, he realised that the children of London's

East End needed help as much as the Chinese. He began by starting a 'ragged' school in the evenings to teach children who would otherwise have no education. One evening when it was time to close the school, Jim Jarvis begged to be allowed to stay in the warm. Barnado tried to send him home but Jim told him he had no home and no parents. Barnado took Jim back to his own lodgings and fed him. Jim showed Barnado the place in the rag market where he slept among many other homeless boys. Soon Barnado was paying for the lodging of several boys and his friends began to help him with gifts of money.

In 1870 an MP gave Dr Barnado enough money to start a proper home for the boys and he opened his first orphanage in Stepney. His rule was that no destitute child should ever be refused admission and from this beginning his great network of orphanages grew. At the time of his death 59,000 children had been taken into his homes.

The first Boy Scouts

The first four boys to be enrolled in the Boy Scouts were brothers, the sons of Lord Rodney who, with some members of the Boys Brigade, were taken to camp on Brownsea Island off the Dorset coast in 1907 by Robert Baden-Powell. He took them as an experiment to see how his ideas about tracking, camping, signalling and learning to be self-sufficient which he had developed in the army would appeal to boys. It was so successful that Baden-Powell decided to start the Scout movement proper. The first Jamboree was held in 1908 and was attended by 11,000 Scouts.

The first Girl Scout

The first Girl Scout was Alison Cargill, a Glasgow schoolgirl who organized a separate patrol of girls who were allowed to become part of the 1st Glasgow Boy Scouts in 1908. By 1909 there were several troops of girls attached to various scout troops and by 1910 there were nearly 6,000 girls enrolled in the Scouts. Baden-Powell had not meant girls to join, but when he saw how popular it was, he arranged for his sister Agnes to organise the Girl Guides.

The girls, much to their annoyance, were made to give up many of the things they most enjoyed – camping, tracking, firelighting – because they were thought to be unladylike and in their place they took up first aid and cooking. However, gradually they won back the right to do the same activities as Scouts.

The fastest Scout-knotter

K. L. Purnell of Calgary, Canada, aged thirteen holds the record for being the fastest person to tie all six of the Scout knots – square knot, sheetbend, sheepshank, clove hitch, round-turn-and-two-half-hitches bowline – each on an individual rope. His time was 10.9 seconds.

The first boy's social club

The first boys to enjoy the benefits of a social club, the forerunners of today's youth clubs, were the boys of Kennington in 1872. The boys played games and were given tea or coffee and bread and butter. Entry was free for boys whose only schooling was at Sunday schools or night schools and also for band boys but all others had to pay a penny a night.

The first children's library

The first library devoted entirely to children's books was set up in 1803 in Salisbury, Connecticut in America. It was set up by a retired bookseller called Bingham who had been deprived of books in his own childhood and so decided to open up a library for children aged between nine and sixteen. It was extremely successful and many children used it.

The first English children's library

The first English children to be able to use a lending library created for them were the children of Nottingham. In 1883 a special branch of the Nottingham library was opened for them.

The youngest Pony Express rider

The youngest rider for the Pony Express, the early American mail service, was William Frederick Cody born in 1846. He began riding for the Pony Express when he was fourteen and set up a record for the fastest non-stop ride of three hundred miles. He later joined the United States Army as a scout and became a buffalo hunter for the Kansas-Pacific railway. He gained the record for the biggest bag of buffalo – sixty-nine killed in one day – and earned himself the nickname Buffalo Bill.

The youngest beauty contest winner

The youngest winner of the Miss America Bathing Beauty Contest was Margaret Gorman who was fifteen when she entered as Miss Washington D.C. in 1921. Margaret, who was still a schoolgirl, was not only the youngest Miss America, she was also the smallest at only five feet and one inch tall and the slimmest with the measurements 30-25-32.

The first baby show

The winner of the first ever baby show was Master Romner of Clark County, Ohio aged ten months. The show was held at Springfield, Ohio in 1845 and his prize was a service of silver plate.

The first registered birth at Somerset House

The first child to have her birth registered at Somerset House was Mary Aaron of Dewsbury, Yorkshire in 1837. Before the Registration Act of 1836, births, deaths and marriages were not registered centrally for the nation but instead baptisms, funerals and marriages were registered in the records of the parish church where they took place.

The first incubator baby

The first premature baby to be kept alive in an incubator and brought safely through infancy was born in 1891 at Nice in France. The inventor of the incubator was Dr Alexandre Lion.

The first birth with anaesthetic

There was a persistent rumour that the first child to be born with the aid of chloroform was christened 'Anaesthesia' but this is not so. The child, who was born in 1847, was Wilhelmina Carstairs, the daughter of a doctor in the Indian Army. The chloroform was administered to her mother in Edinburgh by Dr. James Simpson who pioneered the use of anaesthetics in Britain.

Prince Leopold, Queen Victoria's youngest son was the first member of the royal family to be born with the aid of chloroform in 1853. 'The effect,' wrote the queen in her diary, 'was soothing, quieting and delightful beyond measure.'

The first blood transfusion

The first person to receive a blood transfusion was a fifteen-year-old French boy in 1667 who was given some lamb's blood by Louis XIV's personal doctor. The boy had been bled twenty times to try to reduce his fever and was in danger of dying from loss of blood. Amazingly the boy recovered and survived, although other patients of the king's doctor who were given similar transfusions were not so fortunate. It was not until the nineteenth century that transfusions of human blood were tried and not until the twentieth century that the matching of blood types was properly understood, making blood transfusions safe and successful.

The first insulin treatment

The first person to be treated with insulin for diabetes was fourteen-year-old Leonard Thompson at Toronto General Hospital in 1922. When the boy was admitted to hospital he was so ill that he had little chance of living but with the help of insulin he was afterwards able to lead a normal life.

The first smallpox inoculation

The first English child to be inoculated against smallpox was the young son of Lady Mary Wortley-Montagu, wife of the British Ambassador to the Turkish Court. Lady Mary brought the idea to England where her baby daughter was inoculated in 1721 by the same doctor who had inoculated her son. Lady Mary set the fashion for inoculation and it was because of her influence that the children of the royal family were similarly treated.

The first person to be treated for rabies

The first person to be successfully treated for rabies (an illness contracted from the bite of a mad dog which had almost always hitherto resulted in death) was Joseph Meister, a young boy from Alsace who was brought to Louis Pasteur in 1885. Pasteur had prepared a serum which he was almost sure would work but he had not yet used it. Meister's parents begged him to try to save the boy so Pasteur began the inoculations which cured him. In later years when the Pasteur Institute was set up in Paris, Joseph Meister became its caretaker.

The tomb of the youngest child in Westminster Abbey

The youngest person to have a tomb in Westminster Abbey is Princess Sophia, daughter of James I of England who was born on the 21st June 1606 at Greenwich and who lived only two days. Her little coffin was taken downriver from Greenwich to Westminster Abbey. James commissioned the royal sculptor Nicholas Poutrain to make her a monument, the cost of which was not to exceed £140. The monument, known as the Cradle Tomb, is absolutely delightful. It is a marble cradle with a coverlet trimmed with carved lace and under the canopy you can see the head of the tiny baby wearing a close cap of lace and a ruff. On the back of the cradle are carved the arms of England, Scotland and Ireland.

The statue of the youngest child

The youngest person to have a statue erected to him is the Mannekin-Pis in Brussels, Belgium. It is not known when the statue was erected but he is known affectionately by the Bruxellois as their oldest citizen. He was the two-year-old son of a Brussels burgher who strayed from home and became lost, during which time, his clothes were stolen. He was found after a great hunt through the streets unconcernedly spending a penny in a gutter, quite naked and grinning happily. His thankful father had a statue made of him combined with a fountain so that he could be immortalised exactly as he was found.

People are very fond of the little boy and in the Maison du Roi in Brussels are kept all the suits of clothes which have been presented to him: he has over a hundred and fifty different outfits among them the costumes of a Belgian miner, a Congolese warrior, a Red Indian chief, a Chinese mandarin, uniforms of various regiments of many countries and of several schools, and the strips of several different sports teams. However he never wears any clothes for long: he is usually seen as he was found in his story, naked.

The statue of the youngest child in England

Probably the youngest person in England to have a statue erected to him was George Hunter, a London apprentice who, in the reign of Mary Tudor, was burned for his faith. This obelisk stands at Brentwood in Essex.

The statue of the youngest child in Wales

The youngest person in Wales to achieve a monument was Tommy Jones who had an obelisk erected to his memory on Brecon Beacons. He was age three when he climbed the escarpment and fell to his death.

The statue of the youngest child in Scotland

The youngest people to be commemorated on a monument in Scotland are to be seen on the Faichney Stone at Inverpeffray, Perthshire. The monument was carved in 1707 by a mason to record the birthdays of his ten children and is decorated with their faces.

Another statue to young people in Scotland is the equestrian statue at Hawick in Roxburghshire erected to commemorate the boys of the district who put to flight English marauders in 1514, the year after the Battle of Flodden at which all the grown men of the area had been killed.

The statue of the youngest child in London

The youngest person to whom there is a statue in London is Peter Pan in Kensington Gardens. Peter Pan was J. M. Barrie's most famous fictional character and the hero of the book of the same name. His age is not known because Peter Pan refused to grow up, therefore he is eternal boy, ever young.

The Sparrow Bookshop

Sparrow has a whole nestful of exciting books that are available in bookshops or that you can order by post through the Sparrow Bookshop. Just complete the form below and enclose the money due and the books will be sent to you at home.

THE JELLYBONE GRAFFITI BOOK	Therese Birch	85p
THE BOY WHO WANTED A DOG	Enid Blyton	65p
THE BIRTHDAY KITTEN	Enid Blyton	65p
WORZEL GUMMIDGE AND THE TREASURE SHIP	Barbara E. Todd	85p
THE MIDNIGHT KITTENS	Dodie Smith	80p
A GHOST HUNTER'S HANDBOOK	Peter Underwood	85p

Picture books

IF MICE COULD FLY	John Cameron	£1·25
CRAZY CHARLIE	Ruth Brown	£1·25
K9 AND THE ZETA RESCUE	David Martin	65p
K9 AND THE BEASTS OF VEGA	David Martin	65p
K9 AND THE TIME TRAP	David Martin	65p
K9 AND THE MISSING PLANET	David Martin	65p

Total plus postage

And if you would like to hear more about our forthcoming books write to the address below for the Sparrow News.

SPARROW BOOKS, BOOKSERVICE BY POST, PO BOX 29, DOUGLAS, ISLE OF MAN, BRITISH ISLES

Please enclose a cheque or postal order made out to Arrow Books Limited for the amount due including 8p per book for postage and packing for orders within the UK and 10p for overseas orders.

Please print clearly

NAME _____

ADDRESS _____

Whilst every effort is made to keep prices down and keep popular books in print, Arrow Books cannot guarantee that prices will be the same as those advertised here or that the books will be available.